# Peaceful Piggy Yoga

## Kerry Lee MacLean

Albert Whitman & Company, Morton Grove, Illinois

Also by Kerry Lee MacLean

*Peaceful Piggy Meditation*

Library of Congress Cataloging-in-Publication Data

MacLean, Kerry Lee.
Peaceful piggy yoga / by Kerry Lee MacLean.
p. cm.
ISBN 978-0-8075-6382-3 (hardcover)
1. Hatha yoga for children—Juvenile literature. 2. Swine—Juvenile literature. I. Title.
RJ133.7.M33 2008  613.7'046083—dc22  2007029975

Published in 2008 by Albert Whitman & Company, 6340 Oakton Street, Morton Grove, Illinois 60053-2723.
Published simultaneously in Canada by Fitzhenry & Whiteside, Markham, Ontario.

Printed in the United States of America.
10 9 8 7 6 5 4 3 2 1

The design is by Carol Gildar.

For more information about Albert Whitman & Company,
visit our web site at www.albertwhitman.com.

# How to Use This Book

Yoga is a series of gentle stretches that bring joy and relaxation. You should never stretch muscles to the point of pain, but just enough to feel a nice pull. Try to hold each pose for at least three deep breaths. The Peaceful Piggy yoga series is safe for piggies of all ages. It can be done at home as a nice way to spend time with parents, brothers, and sisters; at school in the classroom (before a test or just to calm and quiet everyone); and just about anywhere with your friends. Regular practice teaches piggies that caring for their minds and bodies feels good—and it can even be fun!

Everyone loves yoga.

Tree Pose

- Start with both feet on the ground and press your hands together.
- Stand on your right leg, and place your left foot on the inside of your right knee.
- Now switch sides, standing on your left leg.
- Each day try inching your foot up a little higher, until your left foot can easily reach the top of your right leg.

The Tree Pose will give you great balance.

Kids do it for fun!

## Candlestick

- To start, lie on your back with your knees bent.
- Lift your legs up toward the ceiling and straighten them.
- Move your arms to hold your lower back firmly with your hands.
- Be sure to support most of your weight on your shoulders—not your neck!
- Try to keep your legs as straight as a candlestick.

This stretches your back.
It's good for the heart, too!

Moms and dads do it for
peace of mind.

- Start by sitting cross-legged.

- Gently pull each foot up onto the opposite thigh. (If this is too hard, try the Half Lotus on page 23.)

- Make sure your back is straight and your chest is open so you can breathe better.

- Keep your eyes open, looking at the ground in front of you.

- Don't think too much; just rest your mind by feeling your breath go in and out, in and out. Count up to ten breaths.

This pose will help you feel a peaceful place inside.

Full Lotus

Football players do yoga to get **stronger.**

Gate Pose

- Kneel on your right knee with the left leg stretched out to the side.
- Make sure your left leg is slightly bent.
- Your left heel should be in line with your right knee.
- Put your left hand on your left ankle.
- Stretch your right arm over your head until you feel a gentle pull.
- Repeat on the other side.

This pose opens your rib cage so you can breathe more deeply.

Ballerinas do yoga for better balance.

Hand-Toe Pose

- Start in the Tree Pose position (page 5).
- Put your left hand on hip—or on the back of a chair, if you need help with balance.
- Grab your right ankle with your right hand.
- Slowly pull your leg up in front of you, then swing it out to the side. It may take some practice before you can extend your leg all the way.
- Repeat on the other side.

This pose gives you excellent balance and makes your stomach strong.

Movie stars do it to look good!

CHINESE THEATER

14

Warrior Pose

- Take a big step to the side with your left foot.
- Turn your left foot so that your toes are facing left.
- Turn your right foot slightly to the left.
- Gently bend your left knee. Keep your right leg straight.
- Make sure your knee doesn't bend too far forward. It should stay directly over your ankle.
- Keep your torso upright and your arms parallel to the ground.
- Repeat on the other side.

This pose makes your legs strong!

Cowboys do yoga after a hard day in the saddle.

## Seated Twist

- Sit with your left knee bent and your right leg extended.
- Put your left hand on the floor behind your back.
- Bring your right elbow over and around your left knee.
- If you can, try twisting further until you can clasp both hands behind your back—but don't overdo it!
- Hold for one to five breaths.

This pose stretches your whole torso, back and front.

Babies do yoga without even knowing it!

**Cobra**

- Plant hands firmly on mat, keeping them close to your body—not stretched out to the side.
- Try to bend your upper back.
- Stretch your chest open as much as you can.
- Breathe very deeply for ten breaths.

This pose opens chest, deepens breathing. It brings oxygen to your brain so you can think more clearly!

You can do yoga anytime, anywhere, any place!

**Lord of the Dance**

- Start by balancing on your left foot. Bend your right leg backward, lifting the right foot up.

- Now reach back and grab your right foot with your right hand.

- Slowly extend your left arm. Try to gently lift your right leg a little higher.

- Repeat on the other side.

- If you have trouble balancing, try facing a wall. You can support yourself against the wall with your forward hand.

Stretches spine and improves balance.

Try yoga at school to get calm and clear before a spelling test.

Half Lotus

- Sit cross-legged.
- Gently stretch one foot up onto the opposite thigh. Leave the other foot on the ground.
- A straight back and open chest make room for lots of breath.
- Rest open eyes on the ground before you.
- Angry thoughts? Let them go. Happy thoughts? Let them go. Just focus on the breath going in and out, in and out.

This pose is one-half the strain of the Full Lotus.

And at bedtime—when you're too *rootin' tootin'* riled up to go to sleep . . .

the Corpse Pose will help you calm down.

Corpse Pose

- Lay flat on your back.
- Close your eyes.
- Rest your arms a couple of inches out from your body. They should be straight but relaxed with palms up.
- No snoring!

This posture is extremely calming. Sweet dreams!

Daily yoga helps piggies concentrate better . . .

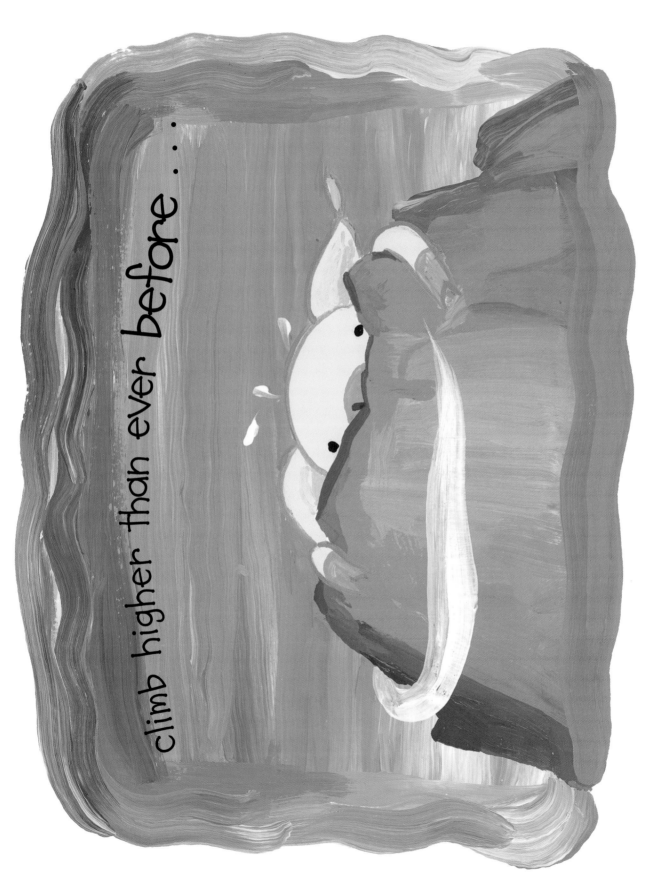

climb higher than ever before . . .

which means peaceful piggies feel

on top of the world!

# The Peaceful Piggy Yoga Series

Try this series of postures!

Candlestick
Page 7

Cobra
Page 19

Tree Pose
Page 5

Seated Twist
Page 17

Warrior Pose
Page 15

To Gregory Michael MacLean, a mad yogi at heart,
and to my peaceful piggy yogin and yogini friends everywhere! —K.M.